YIDDISH PROVERBS

YIDDISH PROVERBS

EDITED BY HANAN J. AYALTI

WITH SIX WOODCUTS BY
BERNARD REDER

SCHOCKEN BOOKS · NEW YORK

TRANSLATED FROM THE YIDDISH
BY ISIDORE GOLDSTICK

First SCHOCKEN PAPERBACK *edition 1963*
Fifth Printing, 1975

CONTENTS

PUBLISHER'S PREFACE   7

PROVERBS   12

INDEX   125

WOODCUTS, BY BERNARD REDER

When a lion sleeps, let him sleep. [89]   *Frontispiece*

A blind horse makes straight for the pit. [3]   15

The girl who can't dance says the band can't play. [111]   35

Each man has a quirk all his own. [340]   53

Love is like butter, it goes well with bread. [357]   87

Pearls around the neck — stones upon the heart. [408] 105

THE PROVERB is the unwritten testimony of a people. It expresses its view, as the case may be, on life and how human beings of all sorts live it, on God and the world, good fortune and bad, youth and old age; it reflects deep-rooted expectations and disappointments. The Yiddish proverb here thus reveals the soul of the Jewish people — more specifically, of the Jewish people of the Eastern European world.

In these pages, the reader will find ample (and at times startling) expression of a paradoxical attitude toward human (and Jewish) existence: a pessimism, general but not so profound as to interfere with an active pursuit of the business of living; a sharp irony which never becomes cruel and destructive; a skepticism which at any moment may turn into faith. Add to the proverbs, in the narrow sense of the word, the large number of witty phrases and puns, and a full panorama of the Yiddish proverb unfolds here.

But here also, side by side with the proverb typical and unique in its Jewishness, stand a large number which instantly recall similar expressions in other cultures and languages, underscoring the existence of basic experiences and reactions common to humans everywhere. We see then that it is not always the subject matter which is characteristic in the proverbial lore of a nation, but the mode of expression, the special turn and twist bestowed on a thought.

For the full, sharp flavor of the proverb in its original spoken form, the Yiddish text* is given, transliterated into the Roman alphabet. In addition, the translation into English tries to retain as much as possible of the characteristics of the original: brevity, the surprising juxtapositions, the play on words and the jingles, the intensity of mood, the occasional exoticism. Only in certain instances did it seem desirable to render in a more general fashion some turn of thought it would be difficult, if not impossible, to understand outside of the special world in which it had its origin.

For the Jewish proverb, there exists an ancient literary tradition, pointing to Israel's love of the brief and pithy expression, and its talent for presenting in the form of pregnant maxims the fruits of human experience, of a vast knowledge of the world.

Aside from the Book of Proverbs as such, the pages of the Bible throughout yield a goodly

* In most instances the text is based on the masterly edition of Yiddish Proverbs by Ignaz Bernstein and B. W. Segel (Frankfort on the Main 1908).

number of proverbial sayings. "The fathers have eaten sour grapes, and the children's teeth are set on edge" (Jer. 31:29 and Ezek. 18:2); "A living dog is better than a dead lion" (Eccles. 9:4).

The main depositories of proverbs in the period after the completion of the Bible are the Book Sirach and the Book of Wisdom. A number of proverbs current in Palestine during that time are quoted in the New Testament. A well-known example: "It is easier for a camel to pass through the eye of a needle, than for a rich man to enter into the kingdom of heaven" (Matt. 19:24).

In the talmudic and midrashic works (the first centuries C.E.), there is recorded a wealth of proverbs (introduced by, "that is it what people say"), employing the language of the masses, Aramaic. Precision of expression is skillfully applied, the satire is clear-cut yet restrained and gentle. "Respect him and suspect him." "Not the mouse is the thief, but the mouse's hole." "A coin in a bottle makes much noise." "He who spits upward will have the spittle falling back in his face."

In the Middle Ages, we find scattered throughout the works of poets and philosophers a great number of epigrams and proverbs, mostly of a didactic and moralistic nature. The influence of

Islamic civilization is clearly discernible. "Your secret is your prisoner; once you reveal it you are its prisoner" — is an example of an Arab proverb which found its way into the Hebrew literature. Another such Arab proverb is the one recorded by Moses ibn Ezra: "Three characteristics has a proverb: few words, right sense, fine image."

Our selection presents the Yiddish proverbs in the variety so typical of this literature. The Index is designed to serve as a guide to the various themes and subject matters. Any attempt at dividing the material itself into logical groups would have interfered with the very nature of the proverb, which resists consequence and subordination. As they appear here, arranged merely in the alphabetical order of the Yiddish original, each proverb can enjoy its genuine isolation, can speak for itself and explain itself, and not be responsible for the one preceding or following it: only stimulate the reader and amuse him.

YIDDISH PROVERBS

A berimer iz gut tsu shlogn. [1]

A beyze tsung iz erger fun a shlekhter hant. [2]

A blinder ferd treft glaykh in grub arayn. [3]

A bruder a soyne iz a soyne afn lebn. [4]

A falshe matbeye farlirt men nit. [5]

A foyler sheliakh gefint ale teyrutsim. [6]

A foyln iz gut tsu shikn nokhn malakh-hamoves. [7]

A fremder bisn shmekt zis. [8]

A fremder nar iz a gelekhter, an eygener — a shand. [9]

A gantser nar iz a halber novi. [10]

Nobody takes a beating like a braggart.

A nasty tongue is worse than a wicked hand.

A blind horse makes straight for the pit.

A brother turned enemy is an enemy for life.

A bad penny never gets lost.

A lazy messenger finds many excuses.

Be sure to send a lazy man for the Angel of Death.

Another man's morsel tastes sweet.

Another's fool is a joke; your own a disgrace.

A whole fool is half a prophet.

A gast iz vi a regn: az er doyert tsu lang, vert er a last. [11]

A gast oyf a vayl zet oyf a mayl. [12]

A gemakhte makhasheyfe iz erger fun a geborener. [13]

A groysser oylem un nito keyn mentsh. [14]

A guter mentsh gehert oyf dem gutn ort. [15]

A guest is like the rain: when he persists, he is a nuisance.

A guest for one day can see a long way.

A woman turned witch is worse than a born witch.

A great assembly, and not a man in it!

A good man's place is beneath the good earth.

A blind horse makes straight for the pit. [3]

A guter mentsh, nor der beyzer hunt lozt nit tsu tsu'n im. [16]

A guter Yid darf nit keyn briv, a shlekhtn Yidn helft nit keyn briv. [17]

A gutn fraynt bekumt men umzist, a soyne muz men zikh koyfn. [18]

A gutn helft a vort, a shlekhtn helft afile keyn shtekn oykh nit. [19]

A gutn vet der sheynk nit kalye makhn, un a shlekhtn vet der bes-hamedresh nit farikhtn. [20]

A good man indeed, but his vicious dog won't let you near him.

A good man needs no recommendation, it does a bad one no good.

A friend is got for nothing, an enemy has to be paid for.

A word to the good is enough, but even a stick won't help the bad.

The tavern can't corrupt a good man, the synagogue can't reform a bad one.

A halber emes iz a gantser lign. [21]

A hun iz gut tsum esn zalbenand: ikh un dos hun.
[22]

A kalyeke git men gikher a nedove vi a talmid-
khokhem. [23]

A karger tsolt tayerer un a foyler geyt mer. [24]

A kats ken oykh kalye makhn. [25]

A kats meg oykh kukn oyfn keysser. [26]

A khissorn, di kale iz tsu sheyn! [27]

A khoynef tor nit in kaas vern. [28]

A kluger farshteyt fun eyn vort tsvey. [29]

A knoyl hot oykh an ek. [30]

Half a truth is a whole lie.

Two at the feast of the chicken: me and the chicken.

More alms are at hand for a cripple than for a scholar.

The miser pays dearer and the sluggard walks farther.

Even a cat can cross your plans.

Even a cat may look at a king.

Too bad, the bride is so pretty.

A flatterer must not lose his temper.

A wise man hears one word and understands two.

The biggest ball of twine unwinds.

A krankn fregt men, a gezuntn git men. [31]

A lustiger dales geyt iber ales. [32]

A melokhe iz a melukhe, ober men hot nit keyn minut menukhe. [33]

A mentsh darf iber zikh keyn ergers nit hobn vi a mentshn. [34]

A mentsh iz shtarker fun ayzn un shvakher fun a flig. [35]

A mentsh zol lebn shoyn nor fun naygerikayt vegn. [36]

A meshumed iz nit keyn Yid un nit keyn goy. [37]

A moshl iz nokh nit keyn raaye. [38]

A nar darf keyn mosser nit hobn. [39]

A nar geyt in bod arayn un fargest zikh dos ponim optsuvashn. [40]

Ask a sick man, feed a well man.

Poor and gay wins the day.

A job is fine, but interferes with your time.

A man can have nothing worse over him than — a man.

Man is stronger than iron and weaker than a fly.

A man should live if only to satisfy his curiosity.

A convert is no Jew and no Gentile.

"For example" is no proof.

A fool is his own informer.

When a fool goes to the baths, he forgets to wash his face.

A nar geyt tsvey mol dort, vu a kluger geyt nit keyn eyntsig mol. [41]

A nar hot a sheyne velt. [42]

A nar hot kheyrus. [43]

A nar iz tomid a baal-gayve. [44]

A nar ken men nit oysnarn. [45]

A nar vakst on regn. [46]

A nogid kumt op, un an oreman kumt oyf, iz nokh nit glaykh. [47]

A patsh fargeyt, a vort bashteyt. [48]

A sakh Homens un eyn Purim. [49]

A sheyn ponim kost gelt. [50]

A fool takes two steps where a wise man takes none.

The fool's world is a paradise.

A fool may take liberties.

A fool puts on airs.

You can never catch up with a fool in his folly.

A fool grows without rain.

Rich man down and poor man up — they're still not even.

The smart of a blow subsides, the sting of a word abides.

So many Hamans and but one Purim.

A pretty face costs money.

A sheyne velt, a likhtike velt, nor vi far vemen.
[51]

A shlekht vayb iz nokh tomid gerekht. [52]

A shlekhter rod skripet amergstn. [53]

A shlekhter sholem iz besser vi a guter krig. [54]

A shlimazl falt oyfn rukn un tseklapt zikh di noz.
[55]

A shlimazl vandert oys ale lender un kumt aheym
on hoyzn un hemder. [56]

A shlos iz gut nor far an orntlekhn mentshn. [57]

A sho in gan-eydn iz oykh gut. [58]

A shtendiger groshn iz besser vi a zeltener rubl.
[59]

A shverer baytl makht a laykht gemit. [60]

A fair world, a radiant world — but, oh, for whom?

A shrew of a wife may yet be somewhat in the right.

The worst wheel squeaks loudest.

Better a bad peace than a good war.

The shlemiehl lands on his back and bruises his nose.

Who's got no luck goes off to far lands with full haversack, returns without pants or shirt to his back.

A lock is meant only for honest men.

Even one hour of heaven is worth while.

Better a steady dime than a rare dollar.

A heavy purse makes a light heart.

A sod iz keyn brokhe. [61]

A toyber hot gehert, vi a shtumer hot dertseylt, az a blinder hot gezen, vi a krumer iz gelofn. [62]

A toytn beveynt men zibn teg, a nar — dos gantse lebn. [63]

A "toyv làkoyl" iz a "ra làkoyl." [64]

A tserisn gemit iz shver tsum heyln. [65]

A vort iz azoy vi a fayl — beyde hobn groysse ayl. [66]

A Yid az er iz klug, iz er klug, un az er iz a nar, iz er a nar. [67]

A yidishe n'shome ken men nit shatsn. [68]

A yokhid gegn kohol, farlirt ale mol. [69]

Abi gezunt — dos lebn ken men zikh aleyn nemen. [70]

To be in on a secret is to be under no blessing.

A deaf man heard a mute tell how a blind man saw a cripple run.

A dead man is mourned seven days, a fool — his lifetime.

Good fellow to everyone — good friend to no one.

A wounded spirit is hard to heal.

A word and an arrow in this are alike: they both fly apace their target to strike.

A wise Jew is very wise; a foolish one is a fool indeed.

You cannot take the full measure of a Jew.

One against all is certain to fall.

Your health comes first — you can always hang yourself later.

Af a mitsve gefinen zikh a sakh balonim. [71]

Af a nar iz keyn kashye nit tsu fregn un keyn pshat nit tsu zogn. [72]

Af der tir fun derfolg iz ongeshribn "shtup" un "tsi." [73]

Afile az der mentsh zet shoyn dem grub ofn, zol er nit oyfhern tsu hofn. [74]

Ale kales zaynen sheyn, ale meyssim zaynen frum. [75]

Ale kinder zaynen kleynerheyt klug, nor dos rov blaybn baym kindershn seykhl. [76]

Ale shtume viln a sakh redn. [77]

Ale vayber hobn yerushe fun zeyer muter Khave. [78]

Ale Yidn kenen zayn khazonim, ober meystns zaynen zey heyzerik. [79]

An alter fraynt iz besser vi naye tsvey. [80]

One good deed has many claimants.

A fool cannot be questioned or explained.

"Push" and "pull" are written on the door of success.

Right down to the brink of the grave, a man must still hope and be brave.

All brides are beautiful, all the dead are holy.

All children are clever when they are small, but most of them grow no wiser.

They that are mute want to talk most.

All women are heirs to Mother Eve.

Every Jew can be a cantor, but he is usually hoarse.

Better one old friend than two new.

An aynreydenish iz erger vi a kreynk. [81]

An eyzl derkont men on di lange oyern, a nar —
on der langer tsung. [82]

An oks far a groshn — az der groshn iz nito! [83]

An oks geyt keyn Olmuts, un kumt fort tsurik an
oks. [84]

An oks hot a lange tsung un ken keyn shoyfer nit
blozn. [85]

An opgesheylte ey falt oykh nit aleyn in moyl
arayn. [86]

An oylom iz nit keyn goylem. [87]

"Ato b'khartonu mikol hoàmim" — vos hostu
gevolt fun di Yidn? [88]

Az a leyb shloft, loz im shlofn! [89]

Az a nar halt di ku bay di herner, ken zi a kluger
melkn. [90]

An imaginary ailment is worse than a disease.

Tell an ass by his long ears, a fool by his long tongue.

A penny an ox — and if you haven't a penny?

Though the ox go out to Olmuts, he comes home an ox.

Though his tongue be long, the ox can't blow the shofar.

Even a shelled egg won't leap into your mouth.

The masses are no asses.

"Thou hast chosen us from among the nations" — why did You have to pick on the Jews?

When a lion sleeps, let him sleep.

If a fool holds the cow by the horn, a clever man can milk her.

Az a nar shvaygt, vert er oykh gerekhnt tsvishn di kluge. [91]

Az a narishkayt gerot afile amol, iz es fort a narishkayt. [92]

Az a Yid ken nit vern keyn shuster, troymt er fun vern a professor. [93]

Az ale zukhn sheyne kales, vu kumen ahin di miesse meydn? [94]

Az an oreman est a hun, iz oder er krank oder di hun. [95]

Az beyde baaley-dinim zaynen gerekht — iz shlekht. [96]

Az der kluger feylt, feylt er vayt. [97]

Az der kop iz a nar, ligt der gantser guf in der erd. [98]

Az der man iz tsu gut far der velt, iz er shlekht far'n vayb. [99]

Az der milner shlogt zikh mitn koymen-kerer, vert der milner shvarts un der koymen-kerer vays. [100]

When a fool holds his tongue, he too is thought clever.

Though folly succeed, it is still folly.

When a Jew can't be a cobbler, he dreams of being a professor.

With all the world looking for pretty brides, what becomes of the homely girls?

When a poor man gets to eat a chicken, one of them is sick.

When both litigants are right, justice makes a sorry sight.

When a wise man errs, he errs badly.

When the head is a fool, the whole body is done for.

A man who's too good for the world is no good to his wife.

When the miller fights with the chimney sweep, the miller gets black and the chimney sweep white.

Az der oks falt, sharfn ale di messer. [101]

Az der oyrakh hust, felt im a lefl. [102]

Az der soyne falt, tor men zikh nit freyen, (ober men heybt im nit oyf). [103]

Az der talmid iz a voyler, iz der rebi oykh a voyler. [104]

Az der tate sheynkt dem zun, lakhn beyde — az der zun sheynkt den tatn, veynen beyde. [105]

When the ox stumbles, all whet their knives.

When the guest coughs, he wants a spoon.

"Rejoice not at thine enemy's fall" — but don't pick him up either.

If the pupil is good, then the master is praised.

When a father gives to his son, both laugh; when a son gives to his father, both cry.

The girl who can't dance says the band can't play. [111]

Az der Yid iz gerekht, khapt er ersht di rekhte klep. [106]

Az der Yid iz hungerik, zingt er, un der poyer shlogt dos vayb. [107]

Az di hatslokhe shpilt, gilt ersht di khokhme. [108]

Az di muter shrayt oyfn kind, "Mamzer!" meg men ir gloybn. [109]

Az dos mazl geyt, kelbt zikh der oks. [110]

When a Jew is right, that's when he gets a right good beating.

When a Jew is hungry, he sings; when a peasant is hungry, he beats his wife.

When luck joins in the game, cleverness scores double.

When a mother calls her child "bastard," you can take her word for it.

With luck, even your ox will calve.

Az dos meydl kon nit tantsn, zogt zi — di klezmer
kenen nit shpiln. [111]

Az es iz bashert eynem dertrunken tsu vern, vert
er dertrunken in a lefl vasser. [112]

Az es vert nit besser, vert mimeyle erger. [113]

Az Got git broyt, gibn mentshn puter. [114]

Az Got vil eynem dos harts opshtoysn, git er im a
groysn seykhl. [115]

Az Got vil, shist a bezim oykh. [116]

Az Got vil shtrofn an am-ho'orets, leygt er im a
loshn-koydesh vort in moyl arayn. [117]

Az Got zol voynen oyf der erd, voltn im di
mentshn di fenster oysgeshlogn. [118]

Az ikh vel zayn vi er — ver vet zayn vi ikh? [119]

Az me hot a sakh tsu tun, leygt men zikh shlofn.
[120]

The girl who can't dance says the band can't play.

He that is fated to drown will drown — in a spoonful of water.

If things don't get better, depend on it, they will get worse.

If God gives us bread, men will give us butter.

Whom God would sorely vex, he endows with abundant sense.

If God so wills it, even a broom can shoot.

The Lord when he wants to punish an ignoramus, inspires him to mouth some piece of learning.

If God were living on earth, people would break his windows.

If I try to be like him, who will be like me?

When there is much to be done, one goes to sleep.

Az men antloyft far fayer, bagegnt men dos vasser. [121]

Az men brit zikh op oyf heysn, blozt men oyf
kaltn. [122]

Az men darf hobn a meylakh, iz a korek oykh a
meylakh. [123]

Az men dermont zikh on dem toyt, iz men nit
zikhér mitn lebn. [124]

Az men fregt a shayle iz treyf. [125]

Az men geyt glaykh, falt men nit. [126]

Az men geyt tsvishn layt, veys men vos es tut zikh
bay zikh in der heym. [127]

Az men git nit Yankevn, git men Eyssovn. [128]

Az men hot a naye kleyd oyf der vant, iz dos alte
kleyd keyn shand. [129]

Az men hot gelt, iz men i klug, i sheyn, i men ken
gut zingen. [130]

If you run from fire, you run into water.

When you're scalded by the hot, you blow on the cold.

A cork will do for a king, if you need him that badly.

Begin thinking of death, and you are no longer sure of your life.

If there is room for question, something is wrong.

He that walks straight will not stumble.

Mix with the neighbors, and you learn what's doing in your own house.

He who fails his own cause, supports the other's.

With a new dress on the wall, the old is no disgrace at all.

With money in your pocket, you are wise and you are handsome and you sing well too.

Az men hot khassene mitn shver, — shloft men mit dem ber. [131]

Az men hot knekht, iz men a har un shtendig gerekht. [132]

Az men iz beroygez oyfn khazn, entfert men nit keyn "Omen." [133]

Az men iz biz tsvantsik yor a kind, iz men tsu eyn-un-tsvantsik — a beheyme. [134]

Az men iz tsu klug, ligt men gor in der erd. [135]

Az men ken nit aroyf, muz men arunter — az men ken nit ariber, muz men ariber. [136]

Az men ken nit baysn, zol men nit sh'tshiren mit di tseyn. [137]

Az men ken nit iberharn dos shlekhte, ken men dos gute nit derlebn. [138]

Az men ken nit vi men vil, muz men veln vi men ken. [139]

Az men khapt a patsh, bakumt men nokh a soyne dertsu. [140]

If it's the father-in-law you wed, a grizzly bear will share your bed.

If to you the slaves belong, you are master and never wrong.

He that has a grudge against the khazn, also begrudges the "Amen."

A child at twenty is an ass at twenty-one.

He that is too smart is surely done for.

If you can't get up, get down; if you can't get across, get across.

If you can't bite, don't show your teeth.

He that can't endure the bad, will not live to see the good.

If we cannot do what we will, we must will what we can.

Get a box in the ear and you get an enemy for good measure.

Az men khazert tsu fil iber vi gerekht men iz, vert men umgerekht. [141]

Az men krigt zikh mitn rov, muz men sholem zayn mitn sheynker. [142]

Az men kumt iber di planken, bakumt men andere gedanken. [143]

Az men kumt nokh yerushe, muz men oft batsoln kvure gelt. [144]

Az men lebt, derlebt men zikh alts. [145]

Az men lebt on kheshbn, shtarbt men on takhrikhim. [146]

Az men leygt zikh nit gegesn, shteyt men oyf nit geshlofn. [147]

Az men ligt oyf der erd, ken men nit faln. [148]

Az men meynt, genart men zikh. [149]

Az men redt a sakh, redt men fun zikh. [150]

Protest long enough that you are right, and you will be wrong.

Make sure to be in with your equals if you're going to fall out with your superiors.

When the fence is left behind, you'll be sure to change your mind.

Call for the legacy and you may have to pay for the funeral.

If you live long enough, you will live to see everything.

He that lives without account dies without shroud.

If you go to bed without supper, you will rise without having slept.

He that lies on the ground cannot fall.

Surmise is self-deception.

Talk too much and you talk about yourself.

Az men shert di shof, tsitern di lemer. [151]

Az men shikt a nar farmakhn di lodn, farmakht er zey in der gantser shtot. [152]

Az men shpayt der zoyne in ponim, zogt zi az es regnt. [153]

Az men shtoyst dem nar in a shtoysl, zogt er az men meynt gor nit im nor dem fefer. [154]

Az men tantst oyf ale khassenes, veynt men nokh ale meyssim. [155]

Az men tut a shidakh, muz men zen mit vemen men vet zikh dernokh tsegeyn. [156]

Az men vil a hunt a zets gebn, gefint men a shtekn. [157]

Az men vil nit alt vern, zol men zikh yungerheyt oyfhengen. [158]

Az men vil nit dem khazn, heyst er zikh nokh gebn a hoysofe. [159]

Az men vil nokhton laytn, varft men zikh oyf ale zaytn. [160]

When the sheep are sheared, the lambs tremble.

Send a fool to close the shutters, and he closes them all over town.

Spit in a whore's face, and she will say it is raining.

Grind a fool in a mortar, and he says you don't mean him but the pepper.

If you dance at every wedding, you will weep for every death.

Before you marry, make sure you know whom you are going to divorce.

If you're out to beat a dog, you're sure to find a stick.

He that would avoid old age must hang himself in youth.

Just when you'd like the khazn out, he wants his wages up.

Who follows others' every stride, is sure to sway from side to side.

Az men zitst in der heym, tserayst men nit keyn shtivl. [161]

Az men zukht a bodner, gefint men a glezer. [162]

Az men zukht khale, farlirt men dervayle dos broyt. [163]

Az naronim hobn lib zis, hobn di kluge oysgetrakht. [164]

Az oyf dem hartsn iz biter, helft nit in moyl keyn tsuker. [165]

Az tsvey zogn shiker, zol *der driter* geyn shlofn. [166]

Azoy lang men lebt, tor men nit redn; az men shtarbt, ken men nit redn. [167]

Azoy vi di tsaytn azoy di laytn. [168]

Badarf men honig, az tsuker iz zis? [169]

Baym glezl gefint men a sakh gute fraynt. [170]

If you stay at home you won't wear out your shoes.

Look for a cooper and you find a glazier.

Look for fancy bread and you lose the plain.

That fools are fond of sweets is an invention of the wise.

If you are bitter at heart, sugar in the mouth will not help you.

When two say you're drunk, it's time to go to bed.

While you live you dare not speak; when you die, you cannot.

Like times, like men.

What need of honey when sugar is sweet?

Over the bottle many a friend is found.

Baym oyskern di shtub gefint men alts. [171]

Baytog tsum get — baynakht tsum bet. [172]

Besser a guter soyne eyder a shlekhter fraynt. [173]

Besser a loyt mazl eyder a funt gold. [174]

Besser an alter top eyder a nayer sharbn. [175]

Besser an oyfgekumener g'vir, eyder an opge-kumener oysher. [176]

Besser der soyne zol bay mir guts zen, eyder ikh bay im shlekhts. [177]

Besser hot keyn shir nit. [178]

Besser mit a klugn in gehenem eyder mit a nar in gan-eydn. [179]

Besser mit a klugn tsu farlirn, eyder mit a nar tsu gevinen. [180]

When the house is swept, everything turns up.

By day they fight, to bed at night.

Better a good enemy than a bad friend.

Better an ounce of luck than a pound of gold.

Better an old pot than a new potsherd.

It is better to be a parvenu and a millionaire than a fine old capitalist and bankrupt.

It is better for my enemy to see good in me than for me to see evil in him.

Better and better knows no limit.

Hell shared with a sage is better than paradise with a fool.

Better to lose with a wise man than win with a fool.

Besser zikh tsu vintshn, eyder yenem tsu sheltn. [181]

Bezint zikh der khokhem, bezint zikh der nar. [182]

Biz der feter vert moger, geyt der mogerer tsu grunt. [183]

Biz zibetsik yor lernt men seykhl un men shtarbt a nar. [184]

B'mokoym she'eyn ish, iz a hering oykh a fish. [185]

Better to pray for oneself than curse another.

The wise man lays plans, but so does the fool.

Before the fat man grows lean, the lean man wastes away.

Up to seventy we learn wisdom — and die fools.

Where men are scarcer than one could wish, even a herring may serve for a fish.

Each man has a quirk all his own. [340]

Brekht zikh a ring, tsefalt di gantse keyt. [186]

Dem oremans gebrotns shpirt men vayt, dem oyshers toyt hert men vayt. [187]

Dem Yidns simkhe iz mit a bisl shrek. [188]

Der bester shuster fun ale shnayders iz Yankl der beker. [189]

Der dales leygt zikh tsum ershtn oyfn ponim. [190]

Break one link and the whole chain falls apart.

The poor man's roast and the rich man's death are sniffed far off.

A Jew's joy is not without fright.

The best cobbler of all the tailors is Yankel the baker.

Where poverty shows up first is in the face.

Der emes iz der bester lign. [191]

Der emes shtarbt nit, ober er lebt vi an oreman. [192]

Der ershter geviner iz der letster farshpiler. [193]

Der eyzl zol hobn herner, un der oks volt gevust fun zayn koyakh, volt di velt keyn kiem nit gehat. [194]

Der gehenem iz nit azoy shlekht vi dos kumen tsu im. [195]

Der glaykhster veg iz ful mit shteyner. [196]

Der Goy iz tsum goles nit gevoynt. [197]

Der kluger bahalt dem seykhl, der nar vayzt zayn narishkayt aroys. [198]

Der koved iz fun dem vos git im, un nit fun dem vos krigt im. [199]

Der mentsh fort un Got halt di leytses. [200]

Truth is the safest lie.

Truth never dies, but lives a wretched life.

The first winner is the last loser.

If the ass had horns and the ox knew his strength, the world would be done for.

Hell is not so bad as the road to it.

The smoothest way is full of stones.

Gentiles aren't used to Jewish troubles.

A wise man hides his wisdom, a fool reveals his folly.

Honor is from him who gives it, not in him who gets it.

Man drives, but God holds the reins.

Der mentsh iz vos er iz, ober nit vos er iz geven. [201]

Der oreman hot veynig faynt, der raykher hot veyniger fraynt. [202]

Der rebi iz groys, ven er hot a sakh kleyne Yide-lekh. [203]

Der rebi trinkt aleyn oys dem vayn un heyst der-noch di andere freylach zayn. [204]

Der seykhl iz a krikher. [205]

Der shenster koved iz, az men zitst in der heym. [206]

Der sheynker hot lib dem shiker, ober di tokhter vet er im nit gebn. [207]

Der vaytster veg iz der, tsu der keshene. [208]

Der "vio!" helft nit, ven di ferd zaynen pegires. [209]

Der volf hot nit moyre farn hunt, ober es gefelt im nit zayn biln. [210]

A man is what he is, not what he used to be.

The poor man has few enemies, the rich man fewer friends.

He is a giant who has many dwarfs about him.

The rabbi drains the bottle and tells the others to be gay.

Reason is a slowpoke.

There is no greater honor than to stay at home.

The innkeeper loves the drunkard, but not for a son-in-law.

The longest road is that which leads to the pocket.

No use shouting "giddap," when the nag is dead.

The wolf is not afraid of the dog, but he hates his bark.

Der vos vil gayve traybn, muz hunger laydn.
[211]

Der yeytser iz a meytser. [212]

Der Yid hot nor gelt tsu farlirn, un tsayt krank
tsu zayn. [213]

Der Yid shlogt, un shrayt "gevalt!" [214]

Di ergste s'khoyre iz "loy." [215]

Di eyer zaynen take kliger far di hiner, ober zey
vern bald farshtunken. [216]

Di eygene zun makht layvnt vays, un dem tsi-
gayner shvarts. [217]

Di eyzlen zaynen gegangen zukhn herner, un
zaynen tsurik gekumen on oyern. [218]

Di gantse velt shteyt oyf der shpits tsung. [219]

Di kats hot lib fish, nor zi vil di fis nit aynnetsn.
[220]

He that stands upon his pride, has starvation at his side.

Passion is a master.

A Jew has money only to lose, and time only to be sick.

A Jew beats you up and shouts, "Help!"

The worst merchandise is "no."

Eggs may be smarter than hens, but soon begin to smell.

The same sun bleaches linen and blackens gypsies.

The donkeys went forth to find horns and came back without ears.

All the world is on the tip of the tongue.

The cat likes fish but hates to wet her paws.

Di kro flit hoykh un zetst zikh oyf a khazer. [221]

Di letste hemd zol men farkoyfn abi a gvir tsu zayn. [222]

Di libe iz zis, nor zi iz gut mit broyt. [223]

Di oygn zoln nit zen, voltn di hent nit genumen. [224]

Di pen shist erger fun a fayl. [225]

Di pod-panes zaynen erger fun di panes aleyn. [226]

Di shverste melokhe iz leydik tsu geyn. [227]

Di tfile geyt aroyf un di brokhe geyt arop. [228]

Di velt iz nit meshuge. [229]

Ding dir a meshores un tu es dir aleyn. [230]

The crow flies high and alights on a pig.

I'd sell the shirt off my back to be a millionaire.

Love is sweet, but tastes best with bread.

If the eyes didn't see, the hands wouldn't take.

The pen stings worse than the arrow.

Straw bosses are worse than bosses.

The hardest work is to go idle.

Prayers rise and blessings descend.

The whole world isn't crazy.

Hire a servant and do it yourself.

Dort vu men hot dikh lib, gey veynig, vu men hot dikh faynt, gey gor nit. [231]

Dos beste ferd darf hobn a baytsh, der kligster mentsh — an eytse, un di frumste nekeyve — a man. [232]

Dos gan-eydn un dem gehenem ken men hobn oyf der velt. [233]

Dos harts iz a halber novi. [234]

Dos holtsepele shvimt fun oybn. [235]

Dos lebn iz di greste metsie — men krigt es umzist. [236]

Dos lebn iz nit mer vi a kholem — ober vek mikh nit oyf! [237]

Dos oybershte kleyd fardekt di untershte layd. [238]

Dos vereml nart op, un nit der fisher oder di vendke. [239]

Dray zakhn vaksn iber nakht: revokhim, diregelt un meydn. [240]

Go rarely where you are loved, and never where you are hated.

The best of horses needs a whip; the wisest of men, advice; the chastest of women — a man.

Heaven and hell can be had in this world.

The heart is half a prophet.

The crabapple floats on top.

Life is the greatest bargain; we get it for nothing.

Life is a dream — but don't wake me.

The outer dress hides the inner distress.

It is the worm that lures the fish, and not the fisherman or his tackle.

Three things grow overnight: profits, rents, and girls.

Emes iz nor bay Got un bay mir a bisl. [241]

Er hot avekgeganvet dem khumesh mit dem "loy signoyv." [242]

Er hot dos lebn fun Got un dos esn fun mentshn. [243]

Er hot azoy fil gelt, vi a Yid khazeyrim. [244]

Er iz a guter b'tsedek. (b'tsedek is an acrostic, meaning: biz tsu der keshene) [245]

Er iz shuldik Got di neshome un dem katsev dos fleysh. [246]

Er klert, tsi a floy hot a pupik. [247]

Er zukht a p'gime oyf der zeg. [248]

Es batsolt nit der raykher, nor der vos iz shuldik. [249]

Es geyt mir vi a tsadik oyf der velt. [250]

Truth rests with God alone, and a little with me.

Along with breaking the commandment not to steal, he stole the Bible.

He has his life from God and his living from man.

He has as much money as a Jew has pigs.

His charity ends at his pocket.

He owes God for his soul, and the butcher for the meat.

He is wondering if a flea has a navel.

He is looking for a notch on the saw.

It isn't the rich man that pays, but whoever is the debtor.

Things are going well for me, like for a saint in this world.

Es iz laykhter bay andere khesroynes tsu gefinen, vi bay zikh mayles. [251]

Es iz nit azoy gut mit gelt, vi es iz shlekht on dem. [252]

Es iz nit azoy mey'ahavas Mordekhay vi mi'sin-'as Homon. [253]

Es iz nito keyn shlekhter bronfn far a shiker, keyn shlekhte matbeye far a soykher un keyn miesse n'keyve far a noyef. [254]

Es iz nito, mit venem tsum tish tsu geyn. [255]

Es iz shver tsu trogn, un avekvarfn tut bang. [256]

Es ken nit vern tsen, ven eyns iz nito. [257]

Eyder tsu shtarbn fun hunger, iz shoyn besser tsu esn gebrotns. [258]

Eyn Got un azoyfil sonim. [259]

Eyn khokhme v'eyn t'vune — k'neged froy fortune. [260]

It is easier to spot faults in others than virtues in oneself.

A full purse is not so good as an empty one is bad.

Affection moves him less, antagonism more.

There is no bad brandy to a drunkard, no tainted money to a merchant, and no ugly wench to a rake.

Not a soul to sit down and take counsel with!

It's a burden to carry, but a pity to throw away.

You can't get ten from less than one.

Rather than die of hunger, I'd sooner eat a roast.

Only one God and so many enemies.

Whatever your wisdom, whatever your wit, Dame Fortune gives not a fig for it.

Eyn mol iz sheyn, tsvey mol hot nokh kheyn,
dray mol brekht men shoyn haldz un beyn [261]

Eyn nar iz a meyvin afn andern. [262]

Eyn nar ken mer fregn, eyder tsen kluge entfern.
[263]

Eyn nar makht a sakh naronim. [264]

Eyner est kez un der anderer davnt in gantsn
nit. [265]

Eyner hakt holts un der anderer shrayt: Ah!
[266]

Eyner vil lebn un ken nit, der anderer ken — un
vil nit. [267]

Eyzehu giber? Ha'koyvesh a glaykh-vertl. [268]

Far a geshlogenem hunt tor men keyn shtekn
nit vayzn. [269]

Far a tsap hot men moyre fun fornt, far a ferd
— fun hintn, far a nar — fun ale zaytn. [270]

Once gets a cheer; twice, a deaf ear; thrice, a kick in the rear.

One fool can tell another.

One fool can ask more questions than ten sages can answer.

One fool makes fools of many.

Right to the point: one eats cheese and the other altogether doesn't say his prayers.

One chops the wood, the other does the grunting.

One man wants to live but can't, another man can — but doesn't want to.

"Who is a hero?" — he who keeps down a wise-crack.

Don't let a beaten dog see the stick.

Shun a billy-goat's front, a horse's hind, and a fool's every side.

Far an akshn iz keyn r'fue nito. [271]

Far dem emes shlogt men. [272]

Far der tliye hobn mentshn mer moyre vi far Got aleyn. [273]

Far der velt muz men mer yoytse zayn vi far Got aleyn. [274]

Far gelt bakumt men alts, nor keyn seykhl nit. [275]

Far Got hot men moyre — far mentshn muz men zikh hitn. [276]

Faran dare gvirim un fete oreme-layt. [277]

Farkoyf, un hob kharote. [278]

Freg an eytse yenem un hob dayn seykhl bay dir. [279]

Fregt nit dem royfe, nor dem khoyle. [280]

For the disease of stubbornness there exists no cure.

Tell the truth and you ask for a beating.

Men stand in greater fear of the gallows than of God himself.

The world is more exacting than God himself.

Money buys everything except sense.

Fear God, beware of men.

Rich men are sometimes lean and poor men sometimes fat.

Sell and be sorry.

Ask counsel of another, and keep your own wits about you.

Don't ask the doctor but the patient.

Frier zaynen di malokhim arumgegangen oyf der erd, haynt zaynen zey in himl oykh nito. [281]

Frish, un gezunt, un meshuge! [282]

Fun a kargn gvir un a fetn bok genist men ersht nokhn toyt. [283]

Fun a kleyner milkhome vert a groysse mehume. [284]

Fun akshones vegn geyt men amol fun gan-eydn in gehenem arayn. [285]

Fun dem ber in vald zol men dos fel nit far- koyfn. [286]

Fun eyn oks tsit men keyn tsvey feln nit arop. [287]

Fun glik tsum umglik iz a shpan — fun umglik tsum glik iz a shtik veg. [288]

Fun hunger shtarbt men nor in a hunger-yor. [289]

Fun itlekhn hoyz trogt men epes aroys. [290]

Time was when angels walked the earth, now they are not even in heaven.

Hale and hearty — and cracked!

A rich miser and a fat goat are of no use until they are dead.

A petty war may lead to a great upheaval.

Many a man leaves heaven for hell just to be stubborn.

Don't sell the skin off the bear that's still in the woods.

You can't pull two hides off one ox.

From fortune to misfortune is but a step; from misfortune to fortune is a long way.

You can die of hunger only in a year of famine.

If you hobnob with men, no matter who, you can always learn a thing or two.

Fun krume shidukhim kumen aroys glaykhe kinder. [291]

Fun loyter hofenung ver ikh nokh meshuge. [292]

Fun nakhes lebt men nit, fun tsores shtarbt men nit. [293]

Fun sholem vegn meg men afile a lign zogn (ober Sholem tor keyn lign nit zogn!) [294]

Fun vaytn, nart men laytn, fun der nont, zikh aleyn. [295]

Fun yidishe reyd ken men zikh nit opvashn in tsen vassern. [296]

Gadles ligt oyfn mist. [297]

Ganve nit un fast nit. [298]

Geborgter seykhl toyg nit. [299]

Geforn tsu der khassene un fargesn dem khosn in der heym. [300]

Bad matches beget good children.

Overfeed on hope and you'll sicken with madness.

One does not live on joy, nor die of sorrow.

For the sake of good relations one may even lie
(but good relations must not lie).

At a distance you fool others; close at hand, just
yourself.

Ten waters will not cleanse you of Jewish talk.

Pride lies on the dunghill.

Rob not, repent not.

Borrowed sense does one no good.

We went to the wedding, but forgot the bride-
groom at home.

Gelt tsu fardinen iz gringer, vi tsu haltn. [301]

Geshvint iz nor gut floy tsu khapn. [302]

Gey red! — az di tsung iz in goles. [303]

Gezunt vi gezunt — vu nemt men ober bulve?
[304]

Glaykher mit a heymishn ganev eyder mit a
fremdn rov. [305]

Glik on seykhl iz a lekherdiker zak. [306]

Gold laykht aroys fun der blote. [307]

Got aleyn iz nit raykh, er nemt nor bay eynem
un git dem andern. [308]

Got heyst oykh keyn nar nit zayn. [309]

Got hot gegebn dem nar hent un fis, un im gelozt
loyfn. [310]

It is easier to make money than to keep it.

Haste is good only for catching fleas.

Just try and talk when your tongue isn't free.

Never mind my health, but where am I to get potatoes?

Better with a hometown thief than an out-of-town rabbi.

Luck without sense is a bag full of holes.

Gold glitters in the mud.

God has no riches of his own; it's what he takes from the one that he gives to the other.

God never told anyone to be stupid.

God gave limbs to the fool and let him run.

Got hot lib dem oreman un helft dem nogid. [311]

Got hot zikh bashafn a velt mit kleyne veltelekh. [312]

Got iz a foter — dos mazl iz a shtif-foter. [313]

Got iz eyner, vos er tut zet keyner. [314]

Got, sheynk mir an oysreyd! [315]

Got shtroft, der mentsh iz zikh noykem. [316]

Got vet helfn — vi helf nor Got biz Got vet helfn. [317]

Got zitst oybn un port untn. [318]

Got zol ophitn tsu hobn eyn kind un eyn hemd. [319]

Gring tsu zogn, shver tsu trogn. [320]

God loves the poor and helps the rich.

God created a world full of little worlds.

God our Father — fortune our stepfather.

God is one and always was; none can witness what he does.

O Lord, give me a good excuse!

God hands out punishment, man takes revenge.

God will provide — if only God would provide until he provides.

God sits on high and makes matches below.

God save me from having one child and one shirt.

Easy to declare, hard to bear.

Gut iz tsu hofn, shlekht iz tsu vartn. [321]

Gute b'sures hert men fun der vaytns. [322]

"Hakoyl hevel" — un ge'hevel't muz dokh vern. [323]

Halt mikh vi a rov un hit mikh vi a ganev. [324]

Halevay volt es azoy yo geven, vi es vet nit zayn. [325]

Hitn zol men zikh far di fraynt, nit far di faynt. [326]

Hob mikh veynig lib, nor hob mikh lang lib! [327]

Hob nit keyn moyre, ven du host nit keyn ander breyre. [328]

Host du — halt; veyst du — shvayg; kenst du —tu! [329]

Iber di falshe trern kenen shoyn di emesse nit aroyf in himl. [330]

It's good to hope, it's the waiting that spoils it.

Good news is heard from far away.

"All is vanity" — but who can get along without it.

Treat me like a rabbi and watch me like a thief.

Would it were what I know it will not be.

Beware of your friends, not your enemies.

Love me little, but love me long.

Don't be afraid when you have no other choice.

What you have, hold; what you know, keep to yourself; what you can, do.

False tears keep the true ones out of heaven.

Ibergekumene tsores iz gut tsu dertseyln. [331]

Ikh bin mitn porets aderabe-ve'aderabe, nor der porets mit mir iz kider-vider. [332]

Ikh nisht foyl — git er mir a patsh. [333]

Ikh zol handlen mit likht, volt di zun nit unter-gegangen. [334]

In dem shpigl zet itlekher zayn bestn fraynt. [335]

In der yugent a beheyme, oyf der elter a ferd. [336]

In di oygn heyst geredt, hinter di oygn heyst gebilt. [337]

In shlof zindikt nit der mentsh, nor zayne kha-loymes. [338]

Itlekhe shtot hot ir meshugenem. [339]

Itlekher mentsh hot zikh zayn shigoyen. [340]

Bygone troubles are good to tell.

I'm great pals with the chief, but he's at logger-heads with me.

So I come right back at him and — get a sock in the jaw.

If I dealt in candles, the sun wouldn't set.

In the mirror everyone sees his best friend.

Young, a donkey; old, an ass.

What's straight talk to your face is slander be-hind your back.

In his sleep it isn't the man that sins but his dreams.

Every village has its village idiot.

Each man has a quirk all his own.

Itlekher tsad hot a tsad sheknegdoy. [341]

Itlekher Yid hot zayn shulkhon-orukh, (un zayn shigoyen). [342]

Karg bedungen, erlikh batsolt. [343]

Kenen toyre iz nit keyn shter tsu aveyre. [344]

Keyn breyre iz oykh a breyre. [345]

Every part has its counterpart.

Every Jew has his own code of laws (and his own brand of madness).

A hard bargain, but prompt pay.

A man may know his Holy Writ, and yet may grievous sins commit.

No choice *is* a choice.

Love is like butter, it goes well with bread. [357]

Keyner veyst nit, vemes morgn es vet zayn. [346]

Kheyn geyt iber sheyn. [347]

Khutspe gilt! [348]

Kleyne heteyrim bringen groysse yissurim. [349]

Kleyne kinder — kleyne freydn; groysse kinder — groysse zorgn. [350]

No man knows whose morrow it will be.

Charm above beauty.

Cheek helps.

Little indulgences precede great sorrows.

Little children, little joys; big children, big cares.

Kleyne kinder lozn nit shlofn, groysse kinder lozn nit lebn. [351]

Kratsn un borgn iz nor gut oyf a vayl. [352]

Kreplakh in kholem iz nit keyn kreplakh nor a kholem. [353]

Kuk arop, vestu visn vi hoykh du shteyst. [354]

Lang, vi dos yidishe goles. [355]

Laykhter tsen lender eyder eyn mentshn tsu derkenen. [356]

Libe iz vi puter, s'iz gut tsu broyt. [357]

Lign tor men nit zogn, ober dem emes darf men nit zogn. [358]

Loyf nit nokh dem koved, vet er aleyn tsu dir kumen. [359]

Mayne kinder, zaynen Gots vunder. [360]

Small children won't let you sleep, big children won't let you live.

To scratch and to borrow won't help for long.

Dumplings in a dream are not dumplings but a dream.

Look down if you would know how high you stand.

As long as the Jewish Exile.

Ten lands are sooner known than one man.

Love is like butter, it goes well with bread.

You must not tell a lie, but you're not bound to tell the truth.

Don't run after honors and they will come of themselves.

My children, big and small, are prodigies all.

Me darf nit zayn hoykh, me zol zayn groys. [361]

Men bagrist nokh di kleyder, men bagleyt nokhn seykhl. [362]

Men falt nit vayl men iz shvakh, nor vayl men meynt az men iz shtark. [363]

Men ken keyn mentshn nit derkenen, biz men zitst nit mit im oyf eyn fur. [364]

Men ken makhn dem kholem gresser vi di nakht. [365]

Men ken mit im vent aynleygn. [366]

Men tor nit betn oyf a nayem meylakh. [367]

Men veyst nit, far vos Got tsu danken. [368]

Men zol nit gepruvt vern mit dem vos a mentsh ken alts fartrogen. [369]

Men zol tomid betn oyf gute gest. [370]

No need to be tall to be great.

You are ushered in according to your dress; shown out according to your brains.

You don't stumble because you are weak, but because you think yourself strong.

To know a man well, you must ride in the same wagon with him.

One can blow up a dream to be bigger than the night.

You can batter down walls with him.

Never pray for a new king.

We don't know what to thank God for.

Spare us what we can learn to endure.

Always pray for good guests.

Men zol zikh kenen oyskoyfn fun toyt, voltn di oreme layt sheyn parnosse gehat. [371]

"Meshane mokeym, meshane mazl" — amol tsum glik, amol tsum shlimazl. [372]

Mit a Yidn iz gut kugl tsu esn — ober nit fun eyn teler. [373]

Mit emes kumt men far Got. [374]

Mit eyn hant shtroft Got, un mit der anderer bentsht er. [375]

Mit fremde hent iz gut fayer tsu sharn. [376]

Mit fremdn seykhl ken men nit lebn. [377]

Mit lign kumt men vayt, ober nit tsurik. [378]

Mit toyre vert men in ergits nit farfaln. [379]

Mit vos far an oyg men kukt oyf eynem, aza ponim hot er. [380]

If the rich could hire others to die for them, the poor could make a nice living.

"He that changes his place changes his luck" —sometimes for the better, sometimes for the worse.

It's good to feast with your fellow, but not from one plate.

The path of truth leads to God.

God reproves with one hand and blesses with the other.

It is easy to poke the fire with another's hands.

One cannot live by another's wits.

A lie will take you far but will not take you home again.

If you have learning, you'll never lose your way.

As you look at a man, so he appears.

Mitn kop kegn di vant — muz men ober hobn a vant. [381]

Nayn rabonim kenen keyn minyen nit makhn, ober tsen shusters yo. [382]

Nd'an kenen eltern gebn, ober nit keyn mazl. [383]

Nit fil getrakht, abi gut gemakht. [384]

Nit genug vos der nogid iz a nogid, gilt nokh zayn kvitl oykh. [385]

Nit itlekher, vos zitst oybn-on, iz a pan. [386]

Nit keyn groysser khokhem, nit keyn kleyner nar. [387]

Nit mit sheltn un nit mit lakhn, ken men di velt ibermakhn. [388]

Nit yeder iz tsufridn mit zayn ponim, ober mit zayn seykhl iz yeder tsufridn. [389]

Nor bay zayn eygenem tish ken men zat vern. [390]

Knock your head against the wall — but there must be a wall.

Nine rabbis don't make a quorum, but ten cobblers do.

Parents can provide a dowry, but not good luck.

Though little thought, it's still well wrought.

Not only are rich men rich, but their checks are good.

Not all that sit in seats of honor are nobles.

No great sage and no small fool.

Not laughter nor reproof can change the world's warp and woof.

Many complain of their looks, but none of their brains.

You can eat your fill only at your own table.

Oder es helft nit oder men darf es nit. [391]

Oder gor, oder gornit! [392]

"Odom yessoydoy mey'ofor vey'soyfoy ley'ofor
— beyne-le-beyne iz gut a trunk bronfn. [393]

On nissim ken a Yid nit lebn. [394]

Oni v'evyoyn et kompanye. [395]

Orem iz keyn shand — ober oykh keyn groysser
koved nit. [396]

Oyf a fremder bord iz gut zikh tsu lernern shern.
[397]

Oyf a maysse fregt men nit keyn kashe. [398]

Oyf a sheynem iz gut tsu kukn, mit a klugn iz
gut tsu lebn. [399]

Oyf a tserissene frayntshaft ken men keyn late
nit leygn. [400]

It won't help, or else you don't need it.

All or nothing at all.

"For dust thou art, and unto dust shalt thou return" — betwixt and between, a drink comes in handy.

How can a Jew live without a windfall!

Beggar, pauper and company.

Poverty is no disgrace, but no great honor either.

Convenient to learn the barber's trade on the other fellow's beard.

Ask no questions, it's a story.

It is good to look at the fair and to live with the wise.

You can't knit up a raveled friendship.

Oyf a vund tor men keyn zalts nit shitn. [401]

Oyf fremder erd boyt men nit. [402]

Oyf itlekhn terets ken men gefinen a naye kashye. [403]

Oyf nissim tor men zikh nit farlozn. [404]

Oyf "volt-ikh" un "zolt-ikh" borgt men nit keyn gelt. [405]

Oyf yenems simkhe hot men tomid a gutn apetit. [406]

"Oylom ke'minhogoy noyheg" — deriber zet take di velt azoy oys. [407]

Perl oyfn haldz — shteyner oyfn harts. [408]

Pitsh, patsh! ver vemen, veys ikh nit. [409]

Purim iz alts fray, ober nokh purim veyst men dokh ver s'iz a nar. [410]

Don't rub salt into a wound.

One doesn't build on foreign soil.

There is a new question to every answer.

One mustn't depend on miracles.

You can't borrow on "I should" and "I would."

You always have a good appetite at someone else's feast.

"The world goes on its ancient way" — that's why it's in such a mess.

Pearls around the neck — stones upon the heart.

Biff! bang! — but I don't know who socked whom.

On Purim everything goes, but after Purim we know who is a fool.

Raykhe kroyvim zaynen nonte kroyvim. [411]

Rebi Note, hot tomid kharote. [412]

Riboyne-shel-oylom, heyb mikh nit un varf mikh nit. [413]

Riboyne-shel-oylom: kuk arop fun dem himl un kuk dir on dayn velt. [414]

Rot mir gut, nor rot mir nit op. [415]

Shakhne, drey zikh, vet men meynen du handlst. [416]

Sheyn shvaygn iz shener vi sheyn reydn. [417]

Shik dayne oyern in di gassen. [418]

Shlep mikh, ikh gey gern! [419]

Shlimazl, vu geysstu? tsum oreman! [420]

Rich kin are close kin.

Reb Notte concurred, then went back on his word.

Lord of the universe, don't lift me up and don't throw me down.

Lord of the universe, glance down from heaven and take a look at your world.

Advise me well in this matter, but don't advise me against it.

Shakhne, keep moving, so they'll think you are busy.

Better eloquent silence than eloquent speech.

Send your ears into the street.

Pull me, I just love to go.

Bad luck, where to? To the poor man's house!

Shlof gikher, me darf di kishn. [421]

Shtarbt men in der yugnt, iz es oyf der elter vi gefunen. [422]

"Shvaygn iz a tsoym far khokhme" — ober nor shvaygn iz keyn khokhme nit. [423]

S'iz besser a Yid on a bord, eyder a bord on a Yidn. [424]

S'iz di eygene Yente nor andersh geshleyert. [425]

Sleep faster, we need the pillows.

Dying while young is a boon in old age.

"Silence is the fence of wisdom" — but mere silence is not wisdom.

Give me a Jew without a beard rather than a beard without a Jew.

The same old Yente, except for the veil.

Pearls around the neck — stones upon the heart. [408]

Takhrikhim makht men on keshenes. [426]

Toyre kumt nit biyrushe. [427]

Tsdoke zol keyn gelt nit kostn un gmilas-khas-
sodim zoln keyn agmas-nefesh nit farshafn,
voltn geven fil tsadikim. [428]

Tsores mit zup iz gringer tsu fartrogn vi tsores
on zup. [429]

Tsu broyt gefint men shoyn a messer. [430]

Shrouds are made without pockets.

Learning cannot be bequeathed.

If charity cost no money and benevolence caused
no heartache, the world would be full of philan-
thropists.

Worries go down better with soup than without.

If you have the bread, you can always find a
knife.

Tsu fil anives iz a halbe shtolts. [431]

Tsu fil koved iz a halbe shand. [432]

Tsu gut iz umgezunt. [433]

Tsu itlekhn nayem lid ken men tsupasn an altn nign. [434]

Tsu-lib ton kost tomid tayer. [435]

Tsum glik badarf men keyn khokhme nit. [436]

Tsum gutn vert men bald gevoynt. [437]

Tsum shlimazl darf men oykh hobn mazl. [438]

Tsum shtarbn darf men keyn luakh nit hobn. [439]

Tsvey faln tsu last: a nar tsvishn kluge un a kluger tsvishn naronim. [440]

Too humble is half proud.

Too much honor is half a shame.

Too good is bad for you.

Every new song can be sung to an old tune.

Trying to please costs you dear.

It wants no wit to be lucky.

One soon gets used to good things.

Even the luckless need their luck.

You don't need a calendar to die.

Two things are a burden: a fool among wise men,
and a wise man among fools.

Tsvey firer: Yosl-Moyshe firt vasser un Got firt di velt. [441]

Untergenumen heyst — zikh farkoyft. [442]

Veln zayn kliger fun ale — iz di greste narishkayt. [443]

Ven a nar varft arayn a shteyn in brunem, kenen im keyn tsen khakhomim nit aroysnemen. [444]

Ven a shiker hot nit keyn bronfn, redt er khotsh fun bronfn. [445]

Ven a shlimazl koylet a hon — geyt er, dreyt er on a zeyger — shteyt er. [446]

Ven ale mentshn zoln tsien oyf eyn zayt, volt zikh di velt ibergekert. [447]

Ven der ferd volt gehat vos tsu zogn, volt er geredt. [448]

Ven der nar volt nit geven mayn, volt ikh oykh gelakht. [449]

Ven di bobe volt gehat a bord, volt zi geven a zeyde. [450]

Both are carriers: Yosl-Moishe carries water, God carries the world.

Pledge yourself — you'll not be redeemed.

Wanting to be wiser than all is the greatest folly.

Let a fool throw a stone into a well and ten wise men can't get it up again.

When a drunk has no liquor, he at least talks about it.

The shlemiehl kills a rooster — still it hops; he winds up a clock — at once it stops.

If all pulled in one direction, the world would keel over.

If the horse had anything to say, he would speak up.

If he weren't *my* fool, I too would laugh.

If grandma had whiskers, she'd be grandpa.

Ven dos mazl kumt, shtel im a shtul. [451]

Ven es zol helfn Got betn, volt men shoyn tsu-
gedungen mentshn. [452]

Ven freyt zikh Got? — az an oreman gefint a
metsie, un git es op. [453]

Ven Got nemt eynem tsu dos gelt, nemt er im
dem seykhl oykh tsu. [454]

Ven hungert a nogid? Ven der dokter heyst im.
[455]

Ven men darf hobn moyakh, helft nit keyn koyakh. [456]

Ven men fort aroys veyst men, ven men kumt
tsurik veyst men nit. [457]

Ven men lakht, ze'en ale — ven men veynt, zet
keyner nit. [458]

Ver es hot a shem far a frihen oyfshteyer, der
meg biz zeyger tsvelf in bet lign. [459]

Ver es hot di meye, der hot di deye. [460]

When Fortune calls, offer her a chair.

If praying did any good, they'd be hiring men to pray.

What makes God happy? To see a poor devil who finds a treasure and returns it.

When God takes away a man's money, he also deprives him of his sense.

When does a rich man go hungry? When it's doctor's orders.

Where brains need to prevail, mere brawn won't avail.

We know the time of our setting out, but not of our return.

Laugh and everybody sees you, cry and you cry unseen.

He who is known for an early riser may lie abed till noon.

Is he rich? — then he boasts a wealth of notions, too.

Ver es hot gegebn tseyn, der vet gebn broyt.
[461]

Ver es hot kinder in di vign, zol zikh mit der velt
nit krign. [462]

Ver es iz sheyn, ikh bin klug! [463]

Ver es toyg nit far zikh, der toyg nit far yenem.
[464]

Ver es vert umzist beroygez, vert umzist vider
gut. [465]

Verter zol men vegn un nit tseyln. [466]

Vi dem klugn iz biter, iz der nar alts freylakh.
[467]

Vi men halt zikh yungerheyt azoy vert men alt.
[468]

Vi men iz tsu zibn, azoy iz men tsu zibetsik.
[469]

Volt der mentsh nor azoy fil vert geven, vi Got
ken helfn. [470]

He that gave us teeth will give us bread.

He that has children in the cradle had best be at peace with the world.

Let who will be handsome; I am clever.

If he's no good to himself, he's no good to the next fellow.

Angry for no reason is reconciled without cause.

Words should be weighed and not counted.

What saddens the wise man gladdens a fool.

The way you live in your youth will make your age.

As you are at seven, so you are at seventy.

If only man were as worthy of help as God is able to provide it.

Vos der mentsh farshteyt veyniger, iz alts far im besser. [471]

Vos der mentsh ken alts ibertrakhtn, ken der ergster soyne im nit vintshn. [472]

Vos es blaybt iber fun ganev, geyt avek afn tre-fer. [473]

Vos es geyt avek vinter oyf heytsung, geyt avek zumer oyf narishkaytn. [474]

Vos es vet zayn mit kol-Yisroel vet zayn mit reb Yisroel. [475]

Vos eyner hot in zikh, varft er fun zikh. [476]

Vos hert men in yam? — "men khapt fish." [477]

Vos ken men fun an oks farlangen mer vi oksn-fleysh? [478]

Vos klener der oylom, alts gresser di simkhe. [479]

Vos kumt mir aroys fun der guter ku vos git a sakh milkh — az zi shlogt dernokh dos shefl oys. [480]

The less a man understands, the better off he is.

A man's worst enemy can't wish him what he thinks up for himself.

What's left from the thief is spent on the fortune teller.

What we spend on fuel in winter, we waste on nonsense in summer.

Whatever happens to Israel will happen to Mr. Israel.

What's in a man, will out.

What's new at sea? They're catching fish.

What more can you expect from an ox than beef?

The smaller the gathering, the higher the spirits.

What good is the cow that gives plenty of milk and then kicks over the pail?

Vos leynger a blinder lebt, alts mer zet er. [481]

Vos men redt bay tog kholemt zikh bay nakht. [482]

Vos mer gevart, mer genart. [483]

Vos mer goy, alts mer mazl. [484]

Vos shverer men nemt zikh for, alts laykhter helft Got. [485]

Vos toyg der guter kop, az di fis kenen im nit trogn? [486]

Vos toyg di khokhme, az di narishkayt gilt? [487]

Vu ikh zits dort iz di mizrakh-vant. [488]

Yayin-soref iz zayn korev. [489]

Yeder barg-aroyf hot zayn barg-arop. [490]

The longer a blind man lives, the more he sees.

What we speak of by day we dream of by night.

The more you pick and choose, the more you stand to lose.

The more of a heathen, the more good luck.

The harder your undertaking, the easier God's help.

What use is a good head if the legs won't carry it?

What use is wisdom when folly reigns?

Where I sit is the seat of honor.

A bottle of gin is his kith and kin.

Every uphill has its downhill.

Yenems khatoyim kumt keyner nit op — men hot eygene genug. [491]

Yidishe ashires iz vi shney in merts. [492]

"Yoyshev bashomayim yiskhak" — im iz gut tsu lakhn. [493]

"Yoytsey b'khipoyzn," farlirt dos gelt un di hoyzn. [494]

Zey hobn zikh beyde lib — er zikh un zi zikh. [495]

Zey zaynen unzere khakhomim vayl mir zaynen zeyere naronim. [496]

Zayt moykhl, un falt mir mayne trep nit arunter! [497]

"Zibn un zibn iz elf" — un der kop iz ayzn. [498]

Zingen ken ikh nit, ober a meyvin bin ikh. [499]

Zint es iz oyfgekumen dos shtarbn, iz men nit zikher mitn lebn. [500]

No man suffers for another's sins — he has enough of his own.

Jewish wealth is like snow in March.

"He that sitteth in heaven laugheth" — it's easy for him to laugh.

You speed and you spurt, lose money and shirt.

They are madly in love — he with himself, she with herself.

They are our sages because we are their fools.

Go, please — before you go falling down my stairs for me.

"Seven and seven make eleven" — and the head is made of lead.

I can't sing a note, but I know all about it.

Ever since dying came in fashion, life hasn't been safe.

INDEX

INDEX

Ailments and Afflictions   31, 62, 65, 77, 81, 213, 280, 401, 481

Dreams   237, 338, 353, 365, 482

Food and Drink   8, 20, 22, 86, 95, 114, 147, 163, 166, 169, 170, 187, 204, 207, 223, 254, 258, 289, 304, 357, 373, 393, 406, 429, 430, 445, 455, 461, 489

Fortune and Misfortune   3, 15, 25, 49, 55, 56, 58, 74, 86, 89, 101, 108, 110, 112, 113, 121, 136, 138, 139, 148, 151, 165, 174, 183, 193, 200, 238, 258, 260, 269, 288, 293, 306, 308, 313, 317, 322, 325, 331, 334, 346, 363, 369, 372, 375, 381, 383, 404, 408, 413, 420, 429, 436, 438, 446, 451, 454, 457, 461, 473, 484, 485, 486, 490, 493

Friend and Foe   4, 18, 49, 80, 103, 128, 173, 177, 202, 259, 326, 400, 472

God and Man   114, 115, 116, 117, 118, 200, 228, 241, 243, 246, 259, 273, 274, 276, 308, 309, 310, 311, 312, 313, 314, 316, 317, 318, 319, 368, 374, 375, 413, 414, 441, 452, 453, 454, 461, 470, 485, 493

Honor   199, 206, 359, 432, 488

Jews and Non-Jews   37, 67, 68, 79, 88, 106, 107, 188, 197, 213, 214, 296, 342, 355, 373, 394, 424, 475, 484, 492

Love and the Family   27, 52, 76, 78, 94, 99, 105, 107, 109, 131, 156, 172, 207, 216, 223, 232, 240, 254, 291, 318, 319, 327, 350, 351, 357, 360, 383, 411, 425, 462, 495

Man's Nature and His Life   13, 15, 16, 19, 20, 27, 28, 35, 36, 50, 55, 56, 64, 65, 70, 71, 75, 77, 85, 93, 94, 104, 111, 120, 123, 134, 141, 145, 146, 147, 150, 153, 159, 162, 163, 195, 201, 212, 217, 220, 221, 234, 235, 236, 237, 239, 245, 253, 254, 267, 271, 273, 285, 297, 307, 316, 323, 335, 340, 347, 354, 356, 361, 364, 365, 380, 389, 390, 393, 428, 431, 437, 445, 458, 464, 465, 472, 476, 481

Nature of the World   51, 54, 194, 217, 219, 229, 233, 274,
   281, 284, 312, 388, 407, 414, 447

Practical Wisdom   5, 6, 8, 23, 24, 26, 30, 31, 38, 49, 53, 57,
   75, 81, 89, 98, 100, 102, 119, 122, 123, 125, 126, 129, 134,
   137, 140, 143, 144, 157, 169, 171, 175, 178, 186, 209, 215,
   216, 218, 224, 232, 235, 240, 256, 257, 261, 266, 280, 286,
   287, 302, 303, 320, 321, 328, 329, 341, 345, 347, 349, 353,
   381, 384, 391, 401, 402, 403, 417, 418, 430, 433, 434, 435,
   442, 447, 448, 457, 459, 466, 474, 478, 480, 482, 483

Rich and Poor. Work   32, 33, 47, 59, 60, 73, 83, 95, 129,
   130, 174, 176, 183, 187, 190, 202, 208, 222, 227, 230, 244,
   249, 252, 277, 278, 283, 289, 301, 304, 307, 311, 343, 371,
   385, 396, 405, 411, 420, 426, 453, 454, 455, 460, 492

Society. Man to Man   11, 12, 14, 17, 26, 48, 61, 62, 64, 66,
   69, 73, 87, 96, 99, 100, 102, 104, 114, 119, 127, 128, 133,
   142, 155, 159, 160, 161, 166, 168, 170, 181, 185, 186, 203,
   204, 207, 211, 225, 231, 233, 245, 251, 255, 266, 290, 295,
   305, 324, 337, 339, 364, 370, 376, 382, 397, 406, 442, 462,
   479, 491, 497

Speech and Silence   2, 19, 38, 48, 66, 77, 82, 91, 117, 150,
   167, 219, 225, 268, 296, 303, 337, 417, 418, 423, 466

Truth and Falsehood   1, 2, 13, 15, 16, 21, 48, 52, 53, 57, 62,
   64, 96, 97, 128, 140, 146, 191, 192, 212, 219, 224, 225, 242,
   272, 273, 294, 296, 298, 330, 338, 344, 358, 374, 378, 428,
   437

Wisdom and Folly   9, 10, 29, 39, 40, 41, 42, 43, 44, 45, 46,
   63, 72, 82, 84, 90, 91, 92, 93, 97, 108, 115, 117, 125, 135,
   140, 149, 152, 154, 164, 179, 180, 182, 184, 198, 205, 262,
   263, 265, 270, 275, 279, 299, 306, 309, 310, 344, 362, 377,
   379, 387, 389, 399, 410, 423, 427, 436, 440, 443, 444, 449,
   454, 456, 460, 463, 467, 471, 487, 496

Words of Wit   22, 27, 36, 46, 62, 70, 85, 88, 116, 120, 124,
   156, 158, 162, 164, 169, 181, 189, 210, 213, 214, 218, 222,
   223, 224, 228, 241, 242, 245, 246, 247, 248, 250, 258, 260,
   264, 267, 268, 281, 282, 292, 293, 296, 300, 304, 311, 315,
   320, 323, 325, 334, 343, 348, 355, 366, 384, 387, 391, 392,
   395, 398, 407, 409, 412, 415, 416, 419, 421, 424, 425, 433,

441, 447, 448, 450, 455, 471, 474, 477, 478, 489, 493, 497, 498, 499

Worldly Power   26, 34, 132, 137, 203, 226, 332, 367, 386, 460

Youth, Old Age and Death   7, 124, 146, 155, 158, 167, 184, 289, 336, 371, 422, 426, 439, 468, 469, 500